ÉRIC KAYSER'S
NEW FRENCH RECIPES

Translated from the French by Carmella Abramowitz-Moreau
Design: Alice Leroy
Copyediting: Helen Woodhall
Typesetting: Claude-Olivier Four
Proofreading: Penny Isaac

Distributed in North America by Rizzoli International Publications, Inc.

Originally published in French as *Mes recettes: Céréales, Graines et Fruits Secs*
© Flammarion SA, Paris, 2008

English-language edition
© Flammarion SA, Paris, 2008

www.editions.flammarion.com

09 10 11   3 2 1
ISBN: 978-2-0803-0095-9
Dépôt légal: 03/2009

Printed in Slovenia by MKT Print

ÉRIC KAYSER'S
NEW FRENCH RECIPES

Éric Kayser with Yaïr Yosefi
Photography by Clay McLachlan

Flammarion

Contents

Eric Kay

Introduction

I love to knead, shape, and bake bread. But I'm also passionate about all the essential ingredients that go into it, which date back to time immemorial. Today, seeking a healthy and balanced diet, we have rediscovered the virtues of natural ingredients that have undergone little processing. This partially explains why good bread has once again taken its rightful place on our tables.

All nutritionists vouch for the importance of grains, seeds, dried fruit, and nuts to your health. They are naturally rich in a wide range of nutrients and fibers, and therefore are indispensable to a healthy diet. While it's common knowledge that dried fruits and nuts can provide stamina for prolonged effort, how much is known about the benefits of wheat, barley, rye, and oats?

My previous books tied in directly with my work as a baker. The focus was on bread in all its forms. Here, I've created recipes that reflect the new French cuisine and incorporate the seeds, grains, dried fruit, and nuts that I use in my breads.

Each seed and each grain has its own particular flavor and texture, which has been gradually forgotten over the years; you have every reason to bring them back into your cooking! All the recipes here are simple to make, and you'll easily find the ingredients in your favorite stores, organic suppliers, and fine speciality shops. Organic, additive-free, or fair trade products—the choice is yours.

My aim is not to bring back medieval-style, heavy, bland, porridge-style food, but to showcase the unique taste of each component of bread through these delicious recipes for every course of the meal.

Éric Kayser

Grains

"I love grains—their colors,
smells, and tastes intensify
the pleasure of my daily work."

Wheat

Wheat has been a vital crop for many centuries because it is nutritious, versatile, and easy to store. It is believed that wheat was first domesticated from wild grasses about 11,000 years ago, and spread through much of Asia, Europe, and North Africa. The Egyptians made the first raised breads with yeast. Wheat is still one of the world's most important food crops and is, in many respects, at the foundation of western civilization. In its different forms, it continues to play an important role in our daily diet.

It is packed with nutrients as varied as phosphorus, calcium, mineral salts, and proteins (in the form of gluten). Its husk, commonly known as "bran," contains the fibers needed for good digestion.

Wheat germ, rich in Vitamin E, is very popular today as it counters the effects of aging.

The subtle flavors of wheat make it easy to cook with other ingredients. It can be used simply cooked or used as semolina and bulgur. It's important not to overcook it, because this gives it an unpleasant porridge-like consistency.

All bakers, of course, are passionate about the grain they knead daily.

Rye, Oats, and Barley

These three grains have similar histories. They were found in Europe at least since ancient times, and barley was probably the first to be cultivated. The crops were transported to the Americas by Dutch and English settlers. However, over the centuries, farming of these grains diminished, no doubt because they do not lend themselves to bread-making as well as wheat does.

Oats are chiefly grown as cattle feed today. Barley is used to make malt for beer, and rye can be found in the form of dark bread, a perfect accompaniment to seafood.

Yet each of these grains has a completely different nutritional profile. Oats have incomparable nutritional qualities, which is why they are increasingly used in food for infants. Barley, with its crisp taste, and rye, with its more pronounced taste, wealth of minerals, and various types of Vitamin B, are both gradually making a comeback to our plates.

I love to use these three different but complementary grains that are so closely intertwined with the history of Europe.

Corn

Corn originated in the Americas, where it was cultivated in the Pre-Columbian era. Its importation to Europe led to significant changes there. It is rich in starch, phosphorus, and magnesium. Its main advantage is that it grows in poor soil, usually reserved, in France, for vineyards. When corn reached the Old World, south-west France was one of the regions that benefited from this crop. We eat corn grilled and boiled on the cob, puréed, as polenta, and as tacos. In France, it's one of the favorite ingredients in mixed salads. Ground into flour, corn is widely used in cooking. And popcorn is now consumed worldwide.

Although it is decried because so much water is needed to cultivate it, I believe that corn is an essential grain and a source of daily well-being. I love its chameleon nature in cooking: crunchy and refreshing, or creamy and warm.

Buckwheat

In French, buckwheat is known as *sarrasin*, and it's thought that this name may originate from the Arab conquerors (the Saracens) who invaded Southern Europe early in the Middle Ages. Although the exact French etymology is uncertain, the grain originated in Asia, has been cultivated in Europe since the late Middle Ages, and was one of the first crops to be introduced by the Europeans to North America.

In France, the word *sarrasin* conjures up images of the Breton crepe, eaten either with a sweet or a savory filling, and of the bread that owes its unique taste to buckwheat flour combined with wheat.

Quinoa

Quinoa is not a grain, but the seed of a plant related to beets, chard, and spinach. Relatively new in the western world, it has been cultivated in the Andean highlands for over 5,000 years.

Rich in protein, manganese, and iron, quinoa is as interesting from a nutritional point of view as a grain. What's more, it is gluten-free and so is ideal as a tasty foodstuff for the gluten intolerant.

It is now readily available in most natural food stores and some supermarkets. You can create many mouthwatering recipes to bring out its delicious taste. I love this plant, even though I only started working with it recently. It is easily digested, and children take easily to what was once known as the "gold of the Incas," with its healthful nutrients.

Fonio

Fonio is mainly cultivated in West Africa and is little known elsewhere.

From a nutritional point of view, it is similar to rice. Its high carbohydrate content (84 percent) makes it an excellent energy food. It is prepared like pasta and rice.

GLUTEN-FREE CORNBREAD

Yields 2 loaves
Preparation time: 15 minutes
Total cooking time: 55 minutes

A dense, tasty bread that's simple to make and gluten free.

Ingredients

2 cups (600 ml) milk
2 oz. or generous ¼ cup (50 g) finely ground yellow polenta (cornmeal)
10 oz. (300 g) finely ground corn flour
⅔ cup (150 g) unsalted butter
4 eggs, separated
1 packed tablespoon (20 g) yeast
salt

Preheat the oven to 350°F (180°C).

In a saucepan, heat 1 ⅔ cups (400 ml) of the milk. Add the polenta and simmer for 5 minutes. Add a little salt. Slowly whisk in the corn flour, and continue to simmer for another 10 minutes. Remove from the heat and whisk in ½ cup (120 g) butter. Set aside.

In a large mixing bowl, beat the 4 egg yolks with the remaining milk.
Add the yeast and set aside.

Stiffly beat the egg whites.

Stir the egg yolks and milk into the corn mixture.

Spoon one third of the beaten egg whites into the corn mixture, and stir in delicately. Incorporate the remaining two thirds.

Butter 2 loaf pans and pour in the dough. Bake for 40 minutes.

Unmold and allow to cool a little before serving.

BULGUR AND ROASTED BELL PEPPERS

Serves 4
Preparation time: 20 minutes
Resting time: 30 minutes
Cooking time: 35 minutes

Ingredients

1 lb (450 g) coarse bulgur
(cracked wheat)
2 red bell peppers
2 green bell peppers
2 yellow bell peppers
1 cup (250 ml) olive oil
⅓ cup (70 ml) balsamic vinegar
3 garlic cloves, peeled and crushed
1 teaspoon (5 ml) ground cinnamon
salt and pepper

Preheat the oven to 425°F (210°C).

Rinse the bulgur.

Roast the whole peppers, turning them over until the skin starts to darken (approximately 20 minutes). Remove them from the oven and place in a plastic bag. Close the bag and leave for about 30 minutes so that the skin can be removed easily.

Peel the bell peppers and remove the seeds. Cut them into quarters. Marinate in ¾ cup (200 ml) olive oil, the balsamic vinegar, and the salt, pepper, and crushed garlic cloves.

Heat the remaining olive oil in a saucepan over high heat. Add the cinnamon and sauté the bulgur for 2 minutes. Pour in 3 ¼ cups (800 ml) water and season with salt and pepper.

Simmer over medium heat for 10 minutes, stirring frequently, until the bulgur reaches the consistency of couscous.

Place the bulgur in a large salad bowl and arrange the marinated bell peppers around the dish.

Serve as a starter, as a side for grilled meat, or as a vegetarian dish.

Éric Kayser's tip
For even more flavor, roast and marinate the bell peppers a day ahead.

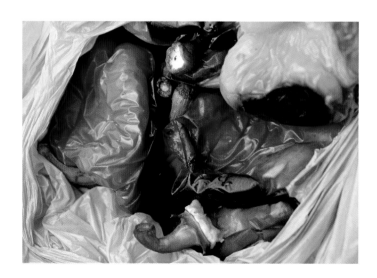

SPELT AND CABBAGE SOUP IN SPELT BREAD

Serves 4
Preparation time: 25 minutes
Soaking time: overnight
Total cooking time: 1 hour 10 minutes

Ingredients

1 lb (500 g) spelt seeds
4 x ½ lb (250 g) spelt loaves
or 1 x 2 lb (1 kg) spelt loaf
4 garlic cloves, peeled
2 onions
1 white cabbage
1 green cabbage
¼ cup (50 g) butter or goose fat
1 marrowbone
1 bouquet garni (bayleaf,
parsley, thyme, and marjoram)
salt and pepper

A day ahead
Rinse the spelt seeds and soak them overnight.

To make the soup
Preheat the oven to 350°F (180°C).
Empty out the soft part of the loaves to make bowls.
Place the loaves in the oven until they are slightly browned. Rub the inside of the loaves with 1 garlic clove.
Peel the onions and slice them. Slice the remaining garlic cloves finely.
Shred the cabbages.
In a pot, over high heat, melt the butter or goose fat. Sauté the onions and garlic.
Add the marrowbone and spelt seeds. Pour in 6 ½ pints (3 liters) water and add the bouquet garni. Simmer at medium heat for 45 minutes.
Stir in the white cabbage and season with salt and pepper. Allow to cook for a further 10 minutes. Add the green cabbage.

Pour into the bread bowls and serve immediately.

Éric Kayser's tip
You'll find spelt seeds in organic and specialty food stores.

DURUM WHEAT RISOTTO
WITH JERUSALEM ARTICHOKES

Serves 4
Preparation time: 20 minutes
Soaking time: overnight
Total cooking time: 1 hour 10 minutes

Ingredients

1 lb (450 g) durum wheat
¾ lb (350 g) Jerusalem artichokes
1 bouquet garni (bay leaves, parsley,
thyme, and marjoram)
2 marrowbones
3 shallots, finely sliced
scant ½ cup (100 g) butter
fleur de sel and pepper

A day ahead

Rinse the durum wheat and soak overnight (no need to soak if using pre-cooked durum wheat).

To prepare

Drain the durum wheat.

Wash the Jerusalem artichokes. Boil them in 2 ¼ pints (1 ½ liters) water together with the bouquet garni and the marrowbones for about 35 minutes, until tender. Drain, filtering the cooking liquid to use for the durum wheat.

Peel the Jerusalem artichokes. Cut 4 into fine slices, ¼ inch (5 mm) thick. Finely chop the others.

In a saucepan, lightly sauté the sliced shallots with ¼ cup (50 g) butter. Add the durum wheat, pour in the reserved cooking liquid, and stir in the chopped Jerusalem artichokes. Cook for 30 minutes until the durum wheat is soft. (If using pre-cooked wheat, follow the instructions on the package.) Drain, incorporate the remaining butter, and season with pepper.

Top with the Jerusalem artichoke slices, season with fleur de sel, and serve immediately.

Éric Kayser's tip

For special occasions, decorate with truffle shavings.

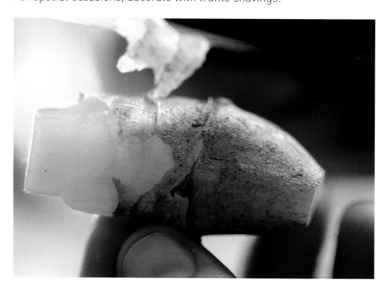

MUSSELS IN WHEAT BEER
WITH LIME

Serves 4
Preparation time: 20 minutes
Cooking time: 10 minutes

Ingredients

4 quarts (4 liters) mussels
1 stalk lemongrass
1 lime, cut into halves
¼ cup (50 g) butter
1 onion, sliced
1 cup (250 ml) white beer (wheat beer)
salt and pepper

Rinse the mussels thoroughly.

Snip the lemongrass into ½ inch (1 cm) slices using a pair of scissors.

Finely slice half the lime (no thicker than ¼ inch or 5 mm) and squeeze the other half, setting aside the juice.

Melt the butter in a large pot and fry the sliced onion. Add the lemongrass, mussels, and beer. Cover and cook for 3 minutes.

Add the lime slices, cover again, and cook for a further 3 minutes. Season with salt and pepper.

Serve the mussels in individual bowls, adding a little lime juice to each one.

Éric Kayser's tip
Choose a good wheat beer (white beer) to make this recipe, as well as to accompany it. The taste of mild wheat pairs perfectly with this refreshing dish.

OPEN-FACED SMOKED CHEESE
AND BASIL-AVOCADO SANDWICHES

Serves 4
Preparation time: 20 minutes
Cooking time: 5 minutes

Ingredients

1 bunch basil
scant ½ cup (100 ml) olive oil
juice of ½ lemon
1 medium-sized avocado pear
2 x 10 oz. (250 g) balls smoked cheese
(Scamorza)
1 x ½ lb (300 g) loaf heavy, dark rye
bread, sliced lengthways
salt and pepper

Pick off the basil leaves and wash and dry them. Process them with the olive oil, salt, pepper, and lemon juice.

Peel the avocado pear and cut into ½ inch (1.5 cm) cubes.
Stir them gently into the basil purée.

Cut each ball of cheese into two, then into slices ¼ inch (5 mm) thick.

Toast the slices of bread. Arrange 5 pieces of cheese on each slice, and spoon over 2 tablespoons of avocado-basil mixture.

Serve with an herb salad seasoned with olive oil and lemon juice.

Éric Kayser's tip
For a more pronounced taste and softer texture, choose a dense, very dark rye bread.

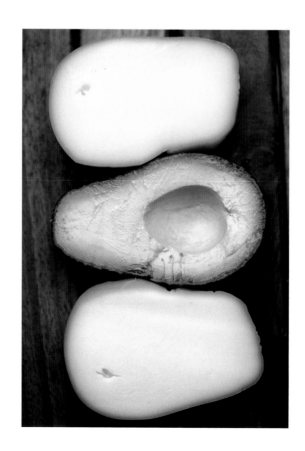

OYSTERS, RYE PILAF, AND SEAWEED

Serves 4
Preparation time: 30 minutes
Soaking time: overnight
Cooking time: 1 hour

Ingredients
5 oz. (150 g) rye seeds
2 oz. (50 g) dried wakame seaweed
24 oysters
1 shallot, finely sliced
¼ cup (50 g) butter
salt and pepper
coarse salt or crushed ice, for serving

A day ahead
Soak the rye seeds in 2 pints (1 liter) water, and the wakame seaweed in 1 ¼ cup (300 ml) water. Leave overnight.

To prepare
Drain the seaweed, keeping the water.

Open the oysters, filter the   through a fine sieve, and set aside.
In a small saucepan, lightly brown the sliced shallot in the butter. Add the drained rye seeds and fry gently for 5 minutes. Pour in the water from the seaweed and the liquid from the oysters. Cover the saucepan and simmer for 50 minutes over low heat, stirring occasionally, until the rye is soft. Season with salt and pepper.
Chop the seaweed and add it to the pilaf.

Place 6 tablespoons coarse salt or crushed ice on each plate and arrange 6 oysters on top. Spoon 1 tablespoon rye pilaf into each oyster.

Éric Kayser's tip
For a refreshing taste, add the juice of half a lemon or 4 tablespoons (60 ml) white wine vinegar to the pilaf when it is almost cooked.

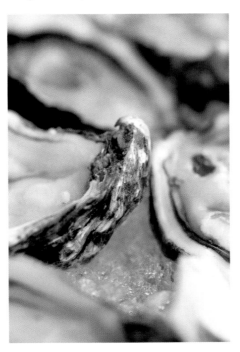

CHICKEN WITH BABY ONIONS AND PEARL BARLEY

Serves 4
Preparation time: 15 minutes
Soaking time: 1 hour
Cooking time: 55 minutes

Ingredients

2 generous cups or 14 oz. (400 g)
pearl barley
1 bunch baby onions
4 cloves garlic
2 sprigs rosemary
2 tablespoons (30 g) butter
4 chicken thighs

Soak the pearl barley in 4 cups water (1 liter) for 1 hour, then drain.

Wash the baby onions and trim them, setting aside the green stalks. Peel the garlic cloves and pick the rosemary leaves off the sprigs.

Melt the butter in a pot and sear the 4 chicken thighs all over until they turn a nice golden color. Add the onions, garlic cloves, and rosemary. Cook for 5 minutes. Stir in the pearl barley, season with salt and pepper, and cover with boiling water. Cook for 45 minutes with the lid on, until the barley is soft.

Snip the onion stalks.

Place one chicken thigh on each plate, together with a few generous spoons of pearl barley. Sprinkle with snipped onion greens.

Éric Kayser's tip
If you like spices, add a tablespoon of turmeric at the same time as the rosemary.

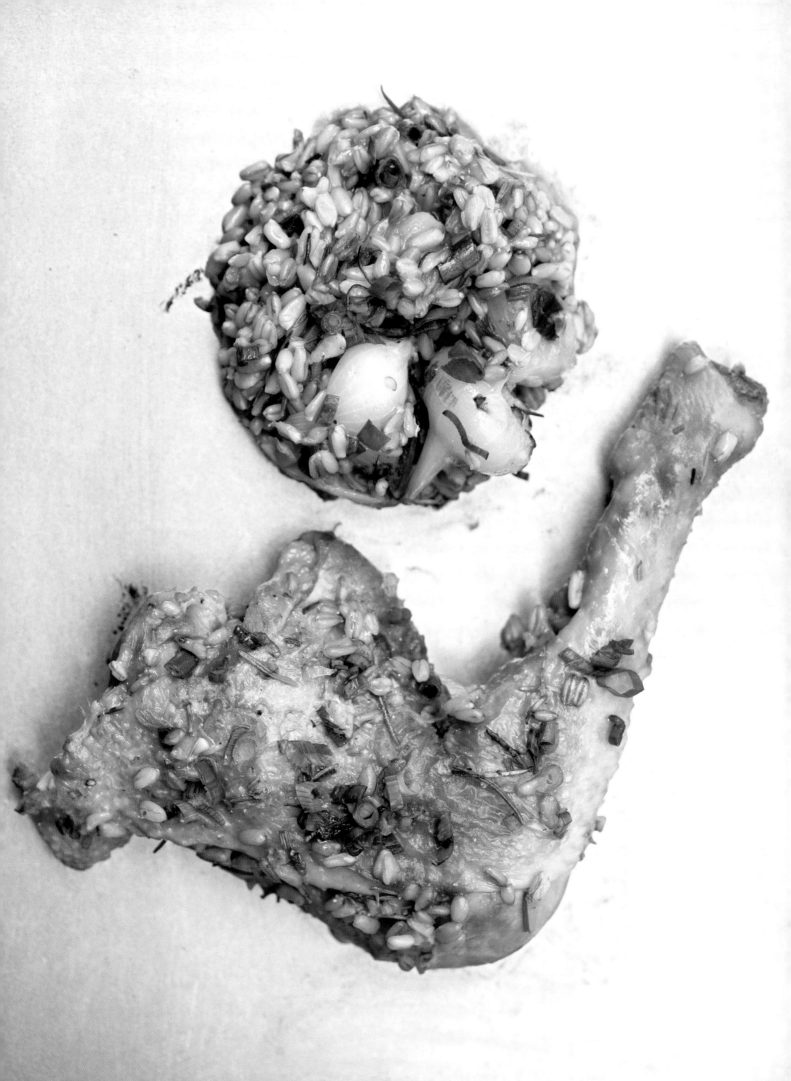

MELON GAZPACHO
AND MINTED BARLEY CARAMEL

Serves 4
Preparation time: 20 minutes
Soaking time: overnight
Cooking time: 35 minutes

Ingredients

1 cup or 7 oz. (200 g) barley groats
1 x 2 lb (1 kg) cantaloupe melon
1 bunch fresh mint
¾ cup (150 g) brown sugar
1 banana

A day ahead
Soak the barley groats in 4 cups (1 liter) water overnight.

To prepare
Peel and seed the melon. Finely process the flesh and chill. Wash the mint leaves, setting aside 2 sprigs.

Cook the barley groats in 4 cups (1 liter) boiling water for 20 minutes. Drain.
In a saucepan, heat the brown sugar with 3 tablespoons (45 ml) water until it becomes a light caramel. Finely dice the banana and add the cubes, together with the 2 reserved sprigs of mint. Incorporate the barley groats and continue cooking for 10 minutes over low heat, stirring frequently. Remove the mint sprigs and allow to cool.

Pour the melon gazpacho into small soup bowls. Add a few teaspoons of barley caramel and decorate with mint leaves.

Éric Kayser's tip
To add an even more refreshing note, add 5 tablespoons (75 ml) mint liqueur to the barley caramel when it is cooked through.

FARMER'S CHEESE
AND OATS WITH MAPLE SYRUP

Serves 4
Preparation time: 10 minutes
Soaking time: 3 hours
Cooking time: 35 minutes
Chilling time: 30 minutes

Ingredients

7 oz. (200 g) oat groats
½ cup (100 g) brown sugar
1 ¼ cup (300 ml) maple syrup
2 tablespoons (30 g) butter
2 ½ cups total (600 ml) farmer's cheese
mixed with a little thick cream,
or fromage blanc

Soak the oat groats in 4 cups (1 liter) water for 3 hours. Drain, discarding the water.

Cook the oat groats in 4 cups (1 liter) boiling water for 20 minutes over medium heat.

In a saucepan, heat the brown sugar with 3 tablespoons (45 ml) water until it becomes a light caramel. Add the drained oat groats and maple syrup. Cook over low heat for a further 10 minutes. Remove from heat and mix in the butter. Chill for about 30 minutes.

To serve, alternate layers of farmer's cheese and oats with maple syrup in individual glasses.

Éric Kayser's tip

This sweet dish makes a perfectly nutritious, tasty breakfast.

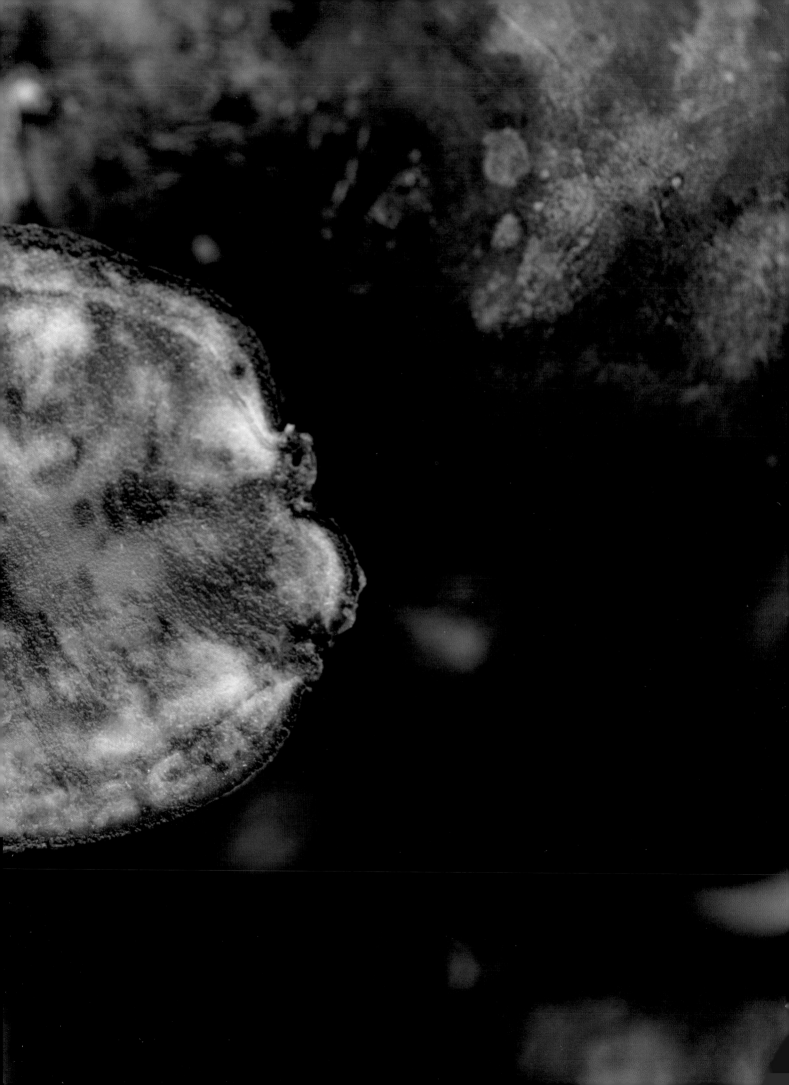

YELLOW POLENTA, CHORIZO, AND ARTICHOKE HEARTS

Serves 4
Preparation time: 25 minutes
Cooking time: 1 hour

Ingredients

1 ½ cups or 7 oz. (200 g) yellow polenta
½ cup (100 g) butter
12 small artichokes
3 ½ tablespoons (50 ml) olive oil
3 oz. (100 g) chorizo, finely sliced
juice of ½ lemon
salt and pepper

Cook the polenta in a saucepan with 3 ¼ cups (800 ml) water over low heat, stirring frequently, until it reaches a creamy texture. Add the butter and season with salt and pepper.

While the polenta is cooking, cook the artichokes in a large pot of boiling water. Drain, remove the fibrous choke, and reserve the hearts, cutting them in two.

Heat the olive oil in a pan and lightly sear the sliced chorizo. Remove the chorizo and sauté the artichoke hearts in the hot olive oil. Pour the lemon juice over the cooked artichoke hearts.

Spoon the polenta into 4 bowls and garnish with the artichoke hearts and crisp chorizo.

Éric Kayser's tip
Add Parmesan shavings or a few drops of balsamic vinegar to each bowl.

CREAMY WHITE POLENTA CAKES
WITH CHOCOLATE CHIPS AND RASPBERRIES

Serves 4
Preparation time: 30 minutes
Cooking time: 50 minutes
Total chilling time: 6 hours

Ingredients

¾ cup or 5 oz. (150 g) polenta,
white if possible
1 ¼ cups (300 ml) milk
⅓ cup (80 g) brown sugar
1 teaspoon ground cinnamon
⅓ cup (70 ml) crème fraîche
2 teaspoons (10g) butter, for greasing
1 ½ oz. or generous ½ cup (45 g)
chocolate chips
3 oz. (100 g) raspberries

In a saucepan, cook the polenta for 50 minutes together with the milk, brown sugar, cinnamon, and 1 ¼ cups (300 ml) water, stirring frequently. Stir in ¼ cup (50 ml) crème fraîche. Grease a baking pan with the butter. With a moistened wooden spoon, spread the polenta onto the pan to a thickness of just under 1 inch (2 cm). Chill for at least 3 hours.

Use a cookie cutter to cut out disks with a 2 ½ inch (6 cm) diameter. Place 1 teaspoon (5 ml) crème fraîche on each disk and cover with chocolate chips. Top with a second polenta disk. Repeat the procedure to make the rest of the individual cakes. Chill for 3 hours.

Garnish with raspberries just before serving.

Éric Kayser's tip
If raspberries are not in season, replace with ripe cubed mango.

MUSCAT WINE JELLY, GRAPES, AND SWEET CORN

Serves 4
Preparation time: 15 minutes
Cooking time: 1 hour 10 minutes
Chilling time: 3 hours

Ingredients

3 oz. (100 g) dried sweet corn kernels
¼ cup (50 g) brown sugar
3 cups (750 ml) Muscato d'Asti, or other slightly sparkling dessert wine
3 oz. (100 g) Muscat grapes
3 ¼ sheets (8 g) leaf gelatin

In a saucepan, cook the corn with the brown sugar and 1 cup (250 ml) wine for 1 hour, until the kernels are tender.

Wash the grapes and cut them in half.

Bring the remaining wine to the boil and remove from the heat. Soak the gelatin sheets in a glass of cold water for a few minutes and then drain them well. Incorporate them into the remaining wine and add the cooked corn kernels. Pour this mixture into large wine glasses, adding a few grape halves to each glass. Chill for at least 3 hours before serving.

Éric Kayser's tip

In summer, use very sweet small husks of sweet corn instead of dried corn kernels. Cook them whole with the sugar and wine.

BUCKWHEAT FRENCH TOAST, SALMON CARPACCIO, AND CREAMED HORSERADISH

Serves 4
Preparation time: 25 minutes
Cooking time: 10 minutes

Ingredients

10 oz. (300 g) salmon fillets (ask your fishseller to skin them)
juice and zest of ½ organic or unsprayed lemon
½ oz. (15 g) horseradish root, grated
½ cup (100 ml) heavy cream or crème fraîche
1 sheet nori seaweed
2 eggs
1 x ½ lb (230 g) buckwheat loaf, sliced
2 teaspoons (10 g) butter
salt and pepper

Cut the salmon into thin strips, ¾ inch x 3 inches (2 cm x 8 cm), and ¼ inch (5 mm) thick. Pour the lemon juice over and sprinkle with the zest.

Set aside 1 heaped tablespoon of the cream. Combine the grated horseradish with the rest of the cream, and season with salt and pepper.

Using a pair of scissors, finely snip the nori seaweed.
Beat the 2 eggs with the tablespoon of cream, and season with salt and pepper.

Cut the slices of bread into sticks and dip them in the egg mixture.
Lightly fry them on all sides in the butter. Spread the creamed horseradish on each breadstick and roll the strips of salmon around them.

Garnish with the sliced seaweed.

Éric Kayser's tip

Dress this up for special occasions: top half of the breadsticks with salmon roe mixed with the zest of half a lemon. Alternate salmon carpaccio fingers with salmon roe fingers on a serving plate.

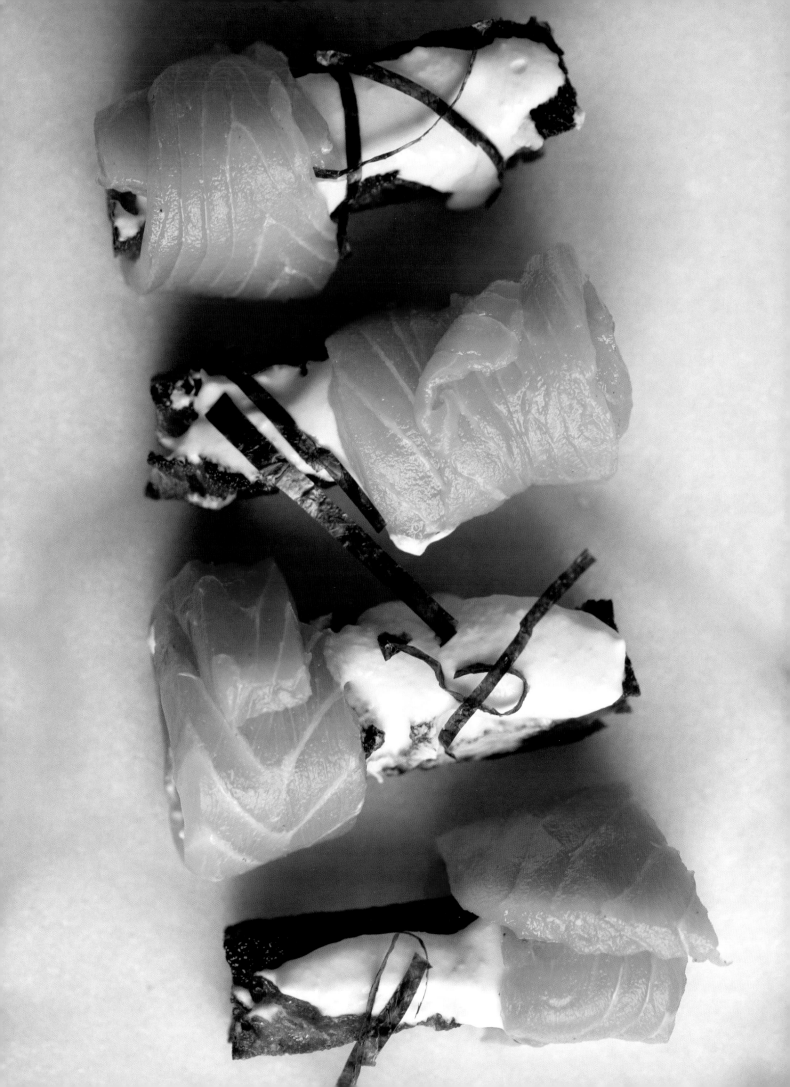

SOBA NOODLES WITH CHICKEN AND BROCCOLI

Serves 4
Preparation time: 20 minutes
Chilling time: 1 hour
Cooking time: 15 minutes

Ingredients

1 bunch cilantro
1 scant cup (200 ml) olive oil
14 oz. (400 g) chicken breast
10 oz. (300 g) broccoli
1 chili pepper (optional),
mild or hot, to taste
1 lb (500 g) soba (Japanese
buckwheat) noodles
3 ½ tablespoons (50 ml) soy sauce
1 lemon
salt and pepper

Wash and dry the cilantro leaves. Process them with half the olive oil and season with salt and pepper.

Cut the chicken breasts into strips ¾ inch (2 cm) thick. Marinate them in the cilantro purée for 1 hour in the refrigerator.

Cut the broccoli into small florets and wash them. Wash the chili if using.
Cook the soba noodles in 8 pints (4 liters) water for the time indicated on the package. Drain.

Heat the rest of the olive oil in a pan and rapidly stir-fry the broccoli and chili. Brown the chicken strips, and deglaze the pan with the soy sauce. Mix the chicken and vegetables with the noodles.

Serve hot in individual bowls with a lemon wedge.

Éric Kayser's tip

If you prefer, replace the cilantro with a bunch of dill.

BUCKWHEAT
WITH MACKEREL AND BEETS

Serves 4
Preparation time: 10 minutes
Cooking time: 40 minutes

Ingredients

4 x ½ lb (250 g) mackerel
1 lb (450 g) cooked beets
3 shallots, sliced
2 garlic cloves, sliced
1 scant cup (200 ml) olive oil
¾ lb (350 g) kasha (buckwheat groats)
⅓ cup (70 ml) balsamic vinegar
salt and pepper

Ask your fishseller to fillet the mackerel.

Peel the beets, and cut them into slices ¼ inch (5 mm) thick.

In a small saucepan, lightly sauté the sliced shallots and garlic cloves in half the olive oil. Add the kasha and gently fry for 5 minutes. Deglaze with the balsamic vinegar. Pour over 2 cups (500 ml) water at room temperature and allow to cook for 20 minutes, stirring from time to time, until the kasha is *al dente*.

Heat the remaining olive oil in a frying pan and rapidly color the mackerel fillets on both sides.

Arrange the fillets on plates with the kasha. Garnish with the sliced beets. Serve immediately.

Éric Kayser's tip
An excellent pairing for this dish is well-chilled Breton apple cider.

GRILLED BUCKWHEAT SANDWICH

Serves 4
Preparation time: 15 minutes
Cooking time: 15 minutes

Ingredients
⅓ cup (70 g) sugar
⅔ cup (150 ml) whipping cream
2 tablespoons (25 g) salted butter
juice of ½ lime
1 orange, preferably a blood orange
1 x ½ lb (270 g) buckwheat loaf, sliced
2 teaspoons (10 g) unsalted butter

In a small saucepan, caramelize the sugar over medium heat, stirring constantly.

In another saucepan, bring the cream to the boil, then add it to the caramel.

Mix thoroughly with the salted butter and lime juice. Chill.

Cut the orange into segments.

Spread the caramel cream over a slice of bread and arrange a few orange segments over this. Cover with another slice of bread, pressing gently.

Heat the unsalted butter in a pan over low heat and color the sandwiches on both sides.

Serve very hot.

Éric Kayser's tip
Cut these sandwiches into sticks to enjoy them as finger food.

RAW TUNA SALAD
WITH FONIO VINAIGRETTE

Serves 4
Preparation time: 20 minutes
Cooking time: 7 minutes

Ingredients
3 oz. (100 g) fonio
2 oz. (50 g) pink radishes
scant ½ cup (100 ml) olive oil
2 tablespoons (30 ml) rice vinegar
1 tablespoon plus 1 teaspoon
(20 ml) soy sauce
1 bunch chives, snipped
4 hearts sucrine lettuce
10 oz. (300 g) ultra-fresh sushi-quality
tuna fillet

For the Fonio Vinaigrette:
Cook the fonio in 1 ¼ cups (300 ml) boiling water for 7 minutes. Drain and chill.
Wash the radishes and grate them.
Combine the oil, vinegar, and soy sauce with the grated radishes, snipped chives, and cooked fonio.

Wash the sucrine lettuces. Cut each one lengthways into 8 wedges.

Cut the tuna into thin slices ¾ inch (2 cm) thick and 2 inches (5 cm) long.

Arrange the lettuce pieces and sliced tuna on a serving dish.
Drizzle with the fonio vinaigrette.

Éric Kayser's tip
The fonio vinaigrette adds a spicy, exotic touch, even to a simple mixed salad.

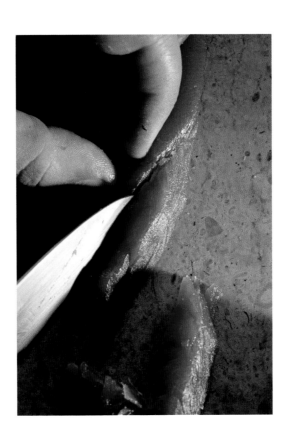

QUINOA WITH THREE ROOT VEGETABLES

Serves 4
Preparation time: 10 minutes
Cooking time: 15 minutes

Ingredients

7 oz. (200 g) quinoa
2 oranges
1 grapefruit
5 oz. (150 g) carrots
5 oz. (150 g) black radish
(daikon or mooli)
5 oz. (150 g) cooked beets
juice of ½ lemon
salt and pepper

Rinse the quinoa. Bring 2 cups (450 ml) salted water to the boil and pour in the quinoa. Cook for 15 minutes at medium heat, until you can see the white germs of the seeds. Remove from heat, cover, and leave to plump for 5 minutes before draining.

Cut 1 of the oranges and the grapefruit into segments.

Peel the root vegetables and chop them very finely. To obtain a semolina texture, you may want to chop each vegetable separately in a food processor. Gently combine the vegetables with the quinoa, the lemon juice, and the juice of the remaining orange. Season with salt and pepper.

Garnish with the orange and grapefruit segments.

Éric Kayser's tip

Replace the salt and pepper with 5 tablespoons of brown sugar to transform this light dish into a dessert.

SAFFRON FONIO COUSCOUS
AND SARDINES

Serves 4
Preparation time: 15 minutes
Cooking time: 20 minutes

Ingredients
4 x 2 oz. (50 g) sardines
½ lb (250 g) flat beans
½ lb (250 g) fine French beans
⅔ cup (150 ml) olive oil
¾ lb (350 g) fonio
1 pinch saffron
salt and pepper

Ask your fishseller to fillet the sardines.

Cook the two types of beans in 4 ¼ pints (2 liters) boiling salted water for about 5 minutes over high heat. They should remain crunchy. Drain, setting aside 4 cups (1 liter) cooking liquid.

Heat 3 tablespoons plus 1 teaspoon (50 ml) olive oil in a large pot. Add the fonio and sauté for 3 minutes. Cover with the 4 cups (1 liter) reserved boiling water, and season with salt and pepper. Add the saffron and continue cooking over high heat, stirring frequently, for 7 minutes, until the fonio has the consistency of couscous.

Heat the remaining olive oil in a skillet and rapidly fry the sardines on both sides.

Combine the fonio couscous with the beans, and top with the sardines.

Éric Kayser's tip
For a distinctively Mediterranean sweet-savory taste, scatter a few raisins on each plate.

EXOTIC FRUIT SALAD WITH QUINOA

Serves 4
Preparation time: 25 minutes
Cooking time: 15 minutes

Ingredients

5 oz. (150 g) quinoa
1 scant cup (200 ml) milk
¼ cup (50 g) brown sugar
1 Victoria pineapple
1 Maya mango
2 persimmons
1 bunch mint
juice of 1 orange

Rinse the quinoa and pour it, together with the milk, into 1 scant cup (200 ml) boiling water. Cook for 15 minutes over medium heat, until you can see the white germs of the seeds. Remove from heat and cover. Leave to plump for 5 minutes, drain, and stir in the brown sugar.

Peel the pineapple and the mango. Dice both fruit, making ½ inch (1.5 cm) cubes.

Cut the persimmons into cubes of the same size.
Wash and dry the mint leaves.

Combine the fruit with the orange juice and quinoa.

Garnish with mint leaves.

Éric Kayser's tip

When they're in season, substitute wild strawberries for the exotic fruits, and add 4 tablespoons (60 ml) thick crème fraîche.

Seeds

"Seeds may be small, but they are rich
in flavor. What I like about them
is their crunchiness and their rustic flavors,
reminiscent of tastes of years gone by."

Sesame

A member of the Pedaliaceae family, sesame originated in the East. This tasty seed is often used to flavor food, whether hot or cold, sweet or savory.

Halva, the Middle Eastern sweet, is made of sesame seeds and sugar. In this region sesame is also used to make tahini, a savory paste eaten with bread, or used as an ingredient to make hummus. In Europe, sesame seeds are added to bread, and in the east they are used in desserts.

Sesame seeds are usually roasted to bring out their flavor. The seeds produce an excellent oil that's delicious in salads. Sesame is rich in fibers, magnesium, and zinc.

I love the distinctive taste of sesame, and I like to decorate breads and cakes with it.

Poppy Seed

This is another interesting seed. The plant, related to the field poppy that produces opium, also gives seeds from which a tasty oil is extracted.

The seeds are rich in proteins, and bring a delightful taste to bread. They are widely used in Eastern Europe and the Middle East. Dark gray-blue, they add a lovely decorative touch to cooking and breads.

I enjoy cooking with poppy seeds: not only are they decorative, but their taste intensifies when they cook. Their spicy note is a perfect match for certain hard cheeses.

Sunflower and Pumpkin Seeds

Because seeds enable plants to reproduce, they are often rich in essential elements.

Sunflower seeds comprise 40–50 percent oil. Over 80 percent of the acids they contain are unsaturated, making their oil a valuable nutritional substance. The seeds are also a source of vitamin E.

Pumpkin seeds, which must be shelled, are rich in proteins, vitamins A, B1, and B2, and contain minerals as well.

These two sorts of seeds are good with drinks, but avoid adding salt, as is often done with pumpkin seeds. A more original idea is to combine the crunchy seeds with vegetables or rice for a delicious toasted note.

PUMPKIN SEED BREAD

Yields 2 x 30 oz. (850 g) loaves
Preparation time: 25 minutes
Resting time: 2 hours 30 minutes
Baking time: 55 minutes

Ingredients

11 oz. (330 g) pumpkin seeds
1 heaped tablespoon (15 g)
granulated sugar
1 cake compressed yeast (25 g)
9 oz. (250 g) rye flour
9 oz. (250 g) stoneground wheat flour
9 oz. (250 g) wholemeal flour
3 teaspoons (15 g) salt
scant ½ cup (100 g) unsalted butter

This bread combines the qualities of different flour types with the mild crunch of fresh seeds.

Preheat the oven to 350°F (180°C).

To bring out the flavor of the pumpkin seeds, roast them in the oven for 10 minutes. Remove, and increase the temperature to 375°F (190°C).

Combine the sugar, ⅓ cup (80 ml) warm water, and the yeast. Allow to rest for 30 minutes.

Combine the different flours and the salt in a mixing bowl.

Incorporate the butter.

Pour the sugar-yeast mixture into the mixing bowl and mix.

Add 2 cups plus 1 tablespoon (520 ml) water. Knead for 10–12 minutes.

Mix in the roasted seeds. Allow to rest for 30 minutes.

Divide the dough between 2 loaf pans. Allow to rise for 1 ½ hours at room temperature.

Make an incision in the top of the bread by slipping a knife rapidly underneath a thin layer of dough.

Place a dish filled with water at the bottom of the preheated oven to reproduce the effect of a hearth deck oven, and bake the loaves for 45 minutes.

Remove from the oven and tip the loaves immediately out of the pans to cool.

BLACK RADISH AND SMOKED TROUT COLESLAW WITH BLACK SESAME

Serves 4
Preparation time: 15 minutes

Ingredients

½ lb (250 g) black radish (daikon or mooli)
7 oz. (200 g) sliced smoked trout
1 tablespoon (15 ml) mayonnaise
3 tablespoons or 1 oz. (30 g) black sesame seeds
juice of ½ lime
salt and pepper

Wash the radishes well, and slice finely. Cut the slices of radish and trout into matchsticks. Mix together delicately to make a coleslaw.

In a small mixing bowl, blend the mayonnaise with the black sesame seeds and lime juice. Add this mixture to the coleslaw.
Season with salt and pepper.

Éric Kayser's tip
This salad is the perfect side dish for a grilled half-lobster.

EGGPLANT CAVIAR
WITH SESAME OIL

Serves 4
Preparation time: 15 minutes
Cooking time: 30 minutes

Ingredients
2 x ¾ lb (350 g) eggplant
1 shallot, snipped
3 tablespoons (45 ml) roasted
sesame oil
5 tablespoons (75 ml) grapeseed oil
1 tablespoon or ⅓ oz. (10 g) black
sesame seeds
rosemary flowers (optional)
salt and white pepper

Preheat the oven to 425°F (210°C).

Wash the eggplants and prick them with a knife. Broil them on a baking tray for 30 minutes, until the core is tender.

Peel them and mash finely. Mix the eggplant caviar with the snipped shallot and the two types of oil. Season with salt and pepper.

Serve warm, sprinkled with black sesame seeds and a few rosemary flowers, if using.

Éric Kayser's tip
For a more marked grilled taste, you can prepare the eggplants by grilling them on a baking tray placed directly on the range over medium heat.

CHICKEN STICKS DIPPED IN BLACK AND WHITE SESAME SEEDS

Serves 4
Preparation time: 15 minutes
Cooking time: 10 minutes

Ingredients

14 oz. (400 g) chicken breast
3 fresh eggs
1 cup (100 g) flour
⅔ cup (100 g) black sesame seeds
⅔ cup (100 g) white sesame seeds
scant ½ cup (100 ml) grapeseed oil
salt and pepper

Cut the chicken breasts into strips ¾ inch (2 cm) thick.

Lightly beat the eggs. Season with salt and pepper.

Roll the chicken strips in the flour. Shake off any excess and then dip them in the beaten eggs. Coat the strips in the sesame seeds: one end in the black seeds and the other in the white seeds.

Heat the grapeseed oil in a skillet and cook the chicken strips, taking care not to burn the sesame seeds. Season with salt and pepper.

Serve in a large dish as finger food.

Éric Kayser's tip
For a dinner buffet, serve this chicken with sliced vegetables and a fonio vinaigrette dip (see vinaigrette recipe p. 53).

SESAME CARAMEL
BANANAS

Serves 4
Preparation time: 10 minutes
Cooking time: 10 minutes

Ingredients

4 bananas, ripe but firm
⅓ cup (75 g) brown sugar
1 scant cup (200 ml) pineapple juice
3 ½ tablespoons or 1 ½ oz. (35 g)
white sesame seeds, untoasted
1 stalk lemongrass

Peel the bananas.

In a skillet over medium heat, heat the brown sugar in the pineapple juice until it caramelizes. Add the sesame seeds, the stalk of lemongrass, and the whole bananas. Remove from heat and gently turn the bananas to coat them in the caramel.

Remove the lemongrass.

Serve immediately with a scoop of vanilla ice cream.

Éric Kayser's tip
Use other fruit when it's in season: mango cubes, apricot halves, or citrus segments.

WHITE ASPARAGUS
WITH PUMPKIN SEED TAPENADE

Serves 4
Preparation time: 10 minutes
Cooking time: 10 minutes

Ingredients
1 bunch flat-leaf parsley
1 bunch cilantro
10 oz. (300 g) pumpkin seeds
scant ½ cup (100 ml) olive oil
1 bunch white asparagus
salt and pepper

Wash and dry the parsley and cilantro leaves, setting aside a few large leaves in the refrigerator.

Lightly color the pumpkin seeds in a skillet with 2 tablespoons (30 ml) of the olive oil. Season with salt and pepper. Set them aside to cool, then chop them finely in a food processor together with the parsley and cilantro leaves, and the remaining olive oil. If the texture is too dense, thin it with a few spoons of water.
Peel the asparagus. Blanch them in boiling water, adding salt after 30 seconds.

Serve the hot asparagus in a tall glass with 2 tablespoons of pumpkin seed tapenade. Garnish with the reserved parsley and cilantro leaves.

Éric Kayser's tip
Spread the pumpkin seed tapenade on a slice of toasted country bread and top with hot goat cheese.

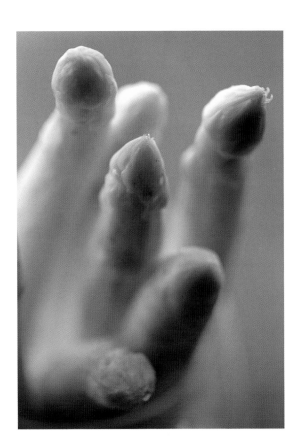

79

BROILED BELGIAN ENDIVE AND TREVISE LETTUCE WITH SUNFLOWER SEEDS

Serves 4
Preparation time: 20 minutes
Marinating time: 30 minutes
Cooking time: 15 minutes

Ingredients
2 oz. (50 g) raspberries
⅔ cup (150 ml) sunflower seed oil
1 ½ oz. (35 g) sunflower seeds
4 tablespoons (60 ml) raspberry vinegar
4 Belgian endives
4 trevise lettuces
salt and pepper

Purée the raspberries: push them through a fine sieve using a spatula.

Combine the raspberry purée with the sunflower seed oil, sunflower seeds, and raspberry vinegar. Season with salt and pepper.

Preheat the oven to 400°F (200°C).

Wash the Belgian endives and trevise lettuces. Cut each into 6 lengthways. Marinate them in the raspberry vinaigrette for 30 minutes.

Place the marinated vegetables on a baking tray and broil for 15 minutes.

Éric Kayser's tip
Serve these sweet-and-sour vegetables hot with sautéed duck breast, or cold with a piece of blue cheese.

NEW POTATOES IN A POPPY SEED AND ROSEMARY CRUST

Serves 4
Preparation time: 15 minutes
Cooking time: 30 minutes

Ingredients
3 sprigs rosemary
1 ½ tablespoons (20 g) butter
1 teaspoon (5 ml) ground piment
d'Espelette (chili pepper from the
Basque region) or other ground
mild chili pepper
generous ½ cup (80 g) poppy seeds
1 lb (450 g) new potatoes
⅔ cup (150 ml) olive oil
fleur de sel

Preheat the oven to 375°F (190°C).

Wash the rosemary leaves.

In a skillet, melt the butter, then add the piment d'Espelette and rosemary leaves. Pour in the poppy seeds and fry gently for 5 minutes.

Wash the potatoes. Cut them in two lengthways, then dip them in the olive oil and fleur de sel. Coat the flat side only with the poppy-seed mixture. Arrange them, round side down, on a baking tray. Cook for 25 minutes.

Éric Kayser's tip
The best potato for this recipe is the *ratte*, an early, firm variety.

ONIONS STUFFED WITH POPPY SEEDS AND PARSLEY

Serves 4
Preparation time: 15 minutes
Cooking time: 25 minutes

Ingredients

1 bunch curly leaf parsley
½ cup or 2 ½ oz. (70 g) poppy seeds
4 large white onions
1 tablespoon (15 g) butter
ground Sichuan pepper
salt

Preheat the oven to 425°F (210°C).

Wash and dry the parsley leaves.

Grind the poppy seeds for 1–2 minutes in a small food processor.

Wash and peel the onions. Wrap each onion in a sheet of aluminum foil.
Broil in the oven for 20 minutes, until tender but still firm.

Empty out the central part of the onions to form small bowls. Chop the onion cores finely
with the parsley, then mix these ingredients with the poppy seeds and butter.
Season with salt and pepper. Fill each onion with the mixture. Bake in the oven
for 5 minutes before serving.

Éric Kayser's tip
Serve this sweet, crunchy vegetable dish with a flavorful meat dish such as Calf's Liver
with Sautéed Jerusalem Artichokes and Walnuts (see recipe p. 108).

APPLE AND POPPY SEED GALETTE

Serves 4
Preparation time: 20 minutes
Total cooking time: 55 minutes

Ingredients
3 Granny Smith apples
scant ½ cup (65 g) poppy seeds
2 tablespoons (30 g) butter
½ cup (110 g) brown sugar
1 egg
2 x ½ lb (250 g) pre-rolled puff pastry

Peel the apples and cut them into small pieces.
In a large saucepan, lightly fry the poppy seeds with the butter and brown sugar for 5 minutes. Add the apples, lower the heat, and cover with the lid. Continue cooking for 15 minutes: the texture should be dense but the apple pieces should not dissolve.

Preheat the oven to 375°F (190°C). Beat the egg.

Cover a baking tray with parchment paper. Cut out 2 puff pastry disks measuring 12 inches (30 cm) in diameter.

Place a disk on the baking tray and cover it with the apple-poppy seed mixture to within ¾ inch (2 cm) of the edge. Place the other disk over this, and press down with your fingers to stick the edges together. Use the blunt side of a knife to make small indentations all the way round the edge, then make incisions in the top pastry disk to allow the steam to escape. Brush with beaten egg and bake for 35 minutes.

Éric Kayser says
In France, we eat this galette at Epiphany, with almond cream filling and a lucky charm hidden in the middle.

Dried Fruit and Nuts

"I have a weakness for these high-energy snacks. They add subtle colors and delicate sweetness to all sorts of breads."

Hazelnuts

Hazelnuts are the fruit of the wild hazelnut tree, known as the filbert in its commercially cultivated variety. The hazelnut tree of the Italian Piedmont region has a particularly good reputation, but Turkey grows two-thirds of the world's production.

Hazelnuts are usually dried before being eaten. They are a popular ingredient for desserts, particularly with fruit and chocolate. They marry well with quite a number of savory dishes, such as delicate fish and meat pâtés. The oil is appreciated for its aroma and delicate flavor.

A good source of energy, hazelnuts are recommended before endurance sport. Its other pluses are its high content of phosphorus, potassium, and calcium.

I like hazelnuts for their slight bitterness and subtle flavor. They add a mild, welcome crunch to dishes.

Walnuts

The fruits of the walnut tree are high in energy, with 51 percent fat content and 11 percent proteins. The fat is mostly polyunsaturated, meaning that walnuts help prevent cardio-vascular disease. Walnuts are rich in vitamins, particularly vitamin E, as well as B3, B5, and B6, and contain mineral salts too. A high-quality oil with a strong taste is extracted from walnuts, but it has a low smoke point and so cannot be used for cooking.

Just like hazelnuts, walnuts marry well with pastries and cakes, as well as terrines. They are a good addition to salads. Their definite bitterness, however, must be attenuated.

I like to use walnuts every day. I can think of no better combination than walnut bread with Comté cheese, along with a small glass of yellow wine from the Jura.

Almonds

The almond is the oleaginous fruit of the almond tree, and its qualities are similar to those of the hazelnut. Almonds are rich in lipids (nearly 50 percent, of which 4 percent is saturated fat, a relatively low figure) and in vitamin E. They are a powerful antioxidant, effective in the prevention of damage from free radicals.

Use almonds fresh or dried, in sweets or in savory dishes, such as trout with almonds. As an ingredient for sweet recipes, almonds go well with chocolate and fruits, in ice creams, creamed desserts, and are used for orgeat syrup. Make versatile use of the texture of almonds by grinding or flaking them, or simply leaving them whole.

I love the taste of almonds. For our traditional Epiphany galette, I sometimes use a little almond cream instead of the usual *frangipane*, and what a treat that is!

Pine Nuts

Pine nuts are a key ingredient in Mediterranean, Middle Eastern, and Indian cuisine. Around the Mediterranean, they grow on the cones of umbrella or parasol pines.

Pine nuts are good eaten whole as a snack, with salads, and in savory dishes, and ground, in sauces. They are one of the basic ingredients of pesto, to which they bring a thick, grainy texture.

Pine nuts contain a very high proportion of fibers, and minerals such as manganese, iron, phosphorus, and copper. They are also rich in vitamin B6. They contain 80 percent unsaturated fatty acids. Pine nuts are often fairly expensive: they are hand picked, and only after 25 years do the trees bear fruit.

I love pine nuts, for they are both delicious and decorative. For me, they symbolize the Mediterranean forest, increasingly endangered by global warming and forest fires.

Raisins

There are several varieties of raisins, including the famous sultana. Like all dried fruits, they lose more than two-thirds of their water in drying, resulting in a concentration of their other elements.

Raisins contain more than four times the carbo-hydrates, minerals, and oligo-elements found in grapes. They are a remarkably high-energy food, and an excellent source of fiber.

Raisins are eaten whole in salads, to accompany meat dishes such as North African tagines, and of course with all kinds of sweet dishes.

As a baker, I associate raisins with the pleasure of making pains aux raisins (raisin brioche pastries) every morning. Their sweet, rich taste also evokes the aromas of a great Sauternes wine.

Dried Plums

The Ente plum tree was probably brought from the east to France during the Second Crusade. From the Middle Ages on, the region of Agen in south-west France has been pro-ducing high-quality prunes. Because they keep so well, sailors took prunes in their provisions. The plum trees used for dried plums were introduced into North America by a Frenchman in the 19th century, and the United States is today the world's largest producer of dried plum, growing an offshoot of la Petite d'Agen. The plums are picked when ripe, then sun dried, or, more frequently, oven dried. It takes 6 lb (3 kg) of fresh fruit to give 2 lb (1 kg) of dried plums.

Dried plums are rich in carbohydrates and are also a good source of iron. They are excellent antioxidants, and their high sorbitol content makes them a widely used laxative.

I love the soft, melting texture of dried plums, which marry equally well with meat dishes as with the most sophisticated desserts.

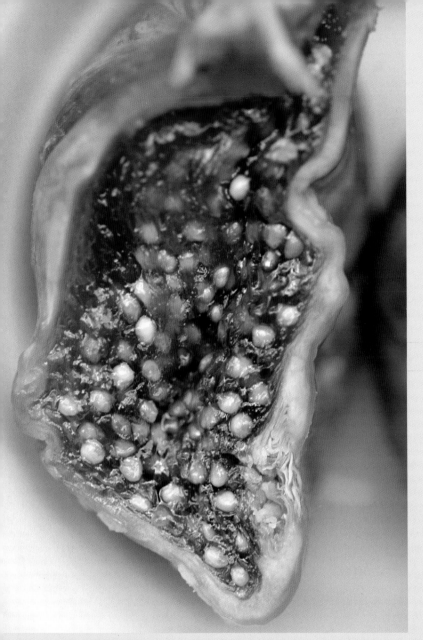

Dried Figs

Fig trees are the oldest known cultivated trees. The fig tree was known to the Ancient Greeks and is frequently mentioned in the Bible. This tree, emblematic of the Mediterranean region, needs only lots of sun to grow, which is why it is such a favorite in the south of France. Today, Turkey is the world's largest producer of this luscious fruit.

A great source of energy, rich in fibers and vitamin B3, dried figs make an ideal snack for long hikes. They are equally good fresh or dried—both kinds are delectable with a large number of recipes, and they marry well with both sweet and savory dishes.

I love these fall fruits for their smooth flavor and lovely colors, which harmonize so well with winter dishes.

Chestnuts

Chestnuts are the fruit of the chestnut tree. They are mainly composed of carbohydrates, and so constitute a high-energy food. They also have a good ration of vitamin C and minerals. Although hardly used in today's diet, chestnuts were vital to mountain civilizations, who could not cultivate grains. Corsica and Sardinia are two notable examples of areas where chestnut flour was used as a staple.

We still use chestnuts at Christmas time for turkey stuffing, and at the beginning of winter in France, it is traditional to glaze chestnuts as a delicacy for the festive season.

I love to work with chestnuts, either puréed or roasted. Protected by their shells, they do not have to undergo pesticide treatments—a real natural treasure!

WALNUT BREAD

Yields 4 loaves
Preparation time: 40 minutes
Chilling time: 2 nights
Total resting time: 2 hours 30 minutes
Baking time: 45 minutes

Ingredients

For the sourdough starter
1 cup (100 g) all-purpose flour

For the bread
5 cups (500 g) all-purpose flour
2 teaspoons (10 ml) salt
3 ½ tablespoons (40 g) sugar
1 ⅔ teaspoons (10 g) yeast
3 ½ tablespoons (25 g) powdered milk
⅓ cup (75 g) butter, softened
2 cups or 8 oz. (230 g) chopped walnuts
2 teaspoons (10 ml) olive oil

A delicious bread, easy to make, with hearty, warm flavors

↻ Two days ahead
In a mixing bowl, combine ¼ cup (50 ml) water with ½ cup (50 g) flour.
Cover with a damp cloth. Every three hours, stir the mixture to activate the fermentation.
Replace the cloth. This should be repeated about 5 times. Chill overnight.

↻ A day ahead
Add ¼ cup (50 ml) water and ½ cup (50 g) flour. Again, stir every three hours and cover each time. Repeat 5 times. Chill overnight again.

✶ To make the bread
The starter is ready. You will need 3 oz. (100 g) to begin making the bread. (With the remaining starter, you can repeat the process indefinitely by adding ¼ cup [50 ml] water and ½ cup [50 g] flour.)

Combine the flour and starter.

Incorporate the salt, sugar, yeast, powdered milk, and butter, ensuring that the salt and yeast don't come into direct contact. Add 1 cup (260 ml) water and mix well.

Add the walnuts and the olive oil.

Stretch out the dough, pulling it toward yourself, so that it gains elasticity.
Fold the dough that you've pulled over the rest of the dough to strengthen its structure and incorporate air into it. Give the dough a quarter turn and repeat the procedure.
For this part of the procedure to be effective, you should spend 15 to 20 minutes stretching and folding.
Cover with a damp cloth, and allow to rest for 1 hour at room temperature.

Use a knife to divide the dough into 4 small loaves, each 10 oz. (310 g).
Flatten the balls with the palm of your hands, without applying too much pressure,
to form a disk.
Take hold of a side of the disk and fold over one-third of the dough.
Press it down over the rest of the dough, applying light pressure with the palms
of your hands.
Take the folded side, and repeat the operation of folding and pressing.
Fold over the last third to obtain the final shape of the bread. Cover and allow
to rest for 1 ½ hours at room temperature.

Preheat the oven to 350°F (170°C). Place a dish of water at the bottom of the oven.
Make incisions on the top of the loaf, letting the blade of the knife penetrate a little
through the surface. You can make up to 5 incisions, but if you prefer, just two 2 ½ inch
(5 cm) incisions on each loaf would be enough because the dough will rise.

Bake for 45 minutes, until the crust is nicely browned. Leave to cool for at least 1 hour
on the oven rack in a dry, well-aired spot.

ROASTED EGGPLANT
WITH HAZELNUT TAHINI

Serves 4
Preparation time: 20 minutes
Cooking time: 15 minutes

Ingredients

2 eggplants
scant ½ cup (100 ml) olive oil
1 bunch basil
scant ½ cup (80 g) whole hazelnuts
juice of ½ lemon
fleur de sel
salt and pepper

Preheat the oven to 425°F (210°C).

Cut each eggplant into 12 thin slices lengthways. Drizzle with olive oil and season with fleur de sel and pepper. Broil in the oven for 15 minutes.

Wash and dry the basil leaves. Chop the hazelnuts and basil in the food processor with 1 scant cup (200 ml) water, salt, pepper, and lemon juice. The mixture should have a creamy, tahini-like texture.

Pour the sauce over the eggplant slices before serving.

Éric Kayser's tip

Serve this as a side dish with grilled lamb chops, drizzled with the same sauce.

GRILLED HAZELNUT
BUTTER SANDWICH

Serves 4
Preparation time: 5 minutes
Cooking time: 10 minutes

Ingredients

1 ½ tablespoons (20 g) butter
2 ½ tablespoons or 1 oz. (25 g)
whole hazelnuts
4 croissants
4 slices of Comté or other
full-flavored hard cheese
white pepper for seasoning

Sauté the hazelnuts in 2 teaspoons (10 g) butter.
Cut the croissants in 2 to make sandwiches.

Place a slice of cheese on the lower half and scatter with hazelnuts. Season with pepper, and cover with the other croissant half.

In the same skillet, over medium heat, melt the rest of the butter until it starts to brown (hazelnut color). Lower the temperature and gently panfry the croissants on each side for 3 minutes.

Serve with cherry tomatoes.

Éric Kayser's tip
This recipe turns day-old croissants into a delicious snack.

HAZELNUT-CHOC ROLL

Serves 4
Preparation time: 10 minutes
Resting time: 2 hours
Chilling time: overnight
Cooking time: 20 minutes

Ingredients

⅓ cup (50 g) whole hazelnuts
1 scant cup (200 ml) whipping cream
7 oz. (200 g) chocolate,
with 70 percent cocoa solids
1 tablespoon (15 g) butter
2 oz. or scant ½ cup (50 g)
unsweetened cocoa powder

↻ A day ahead

Preheat the oven to 325°F (160°C).

Roast the hazelnuts in the oven for 15 minutes.

Heat the cream in a small saucepan over low heat.

Melt the chocolate in a bain-marie. Pour the cream slowly over the chocolate, stirring constantly. Remove from the heat and add the roasted hazelnuts and butter. Allow the ganache to cool for 2 hours, until it becomes compact and elastic.
Pour half the ganache on a sheet of parchment paper, then roll it to form a sausage shape with a 2 inch (5 cm) diameter. Repeat the procedure with the other half of the ganache.

Chill for at least one night.

✳ To assemble

Unwrap the roll from the plastic film, sprinkle with cocoa, and serve.

Éric Kayser's tip

Use a large meat knife to cut the roll and serve the slices with a few teaspoons of custard.

WALNUT TARTLETS WITH BLUE CHEESE AND JURA YELLOW WINE

Serves 4
Preparation time: 25 minutes
Resting time: 15 minutes
Chilling time: 45 minutes
Cooking time: 25 minutes

Ingredients

2 cups (210 g) flour plus a little
extra for the pastry board
1 teaspoon (5 g) salt
scant ½ cup (100 g) unsalted
butter, softened and diced
1 ¼ cups (150 g) walnuts
5 oz. (150 g) Roquefort
or other strong blue cheese
2 eggs
scant ½ cup (100 ml) heavy
cream or crème fraîche
scant ½ cup (100 ml) milk
⅓ cup (75 ml) yellow wine
from the Jura

Sift the flour and the salt through a fine sieve into a mixing bowl. Make a well in the center and add the diced butter. Rub the butter into the flour until crumbs form. Make another well using your hands and pour in ⅓ cup (75 ml) cold water. With the tips of your fingers, knead the dough into a firm ball.

Dust a pastry board with flour and flatten the ball with the palm of your hand. Shape it into a ball again, and repeat the procedure. Wrap the dough in plastic wrap and chill for about 30 minutes.
Remove from the refrigerator and leave at room temperature for 15 minutes. Dust a rolling pin with flour and roll out the dough. Line individual tartlet molds and chill again. Remove from the refrigerator 15 minutes before baking.

Preheat the oven to 350°F (180°C).
Divide the walnuts and the Roquefort cheese equally among the tartlets. Beat the eggs with the cream, milk, and yellow Jura wine, and pour the mixture into the tartlets.
Bake for 25 minutes.

Éric Kayser's tip
If you can't find yellow wine from the Jura region, substitute dry amber sherry.

GREEN ASPARAGUS WITH RADISH AND WALNUT RÉMOULADE

Serves 4
Preparation time: 15 minutes
Cooking time: 10 minutes

Ingredients

1 bunch radishes
¾ cup (85 g) walnuts
2 tablespoons (30 ml) grapeseed oil
⅔ cup (150 ml) heavy cream
or crème fraîche
1 tablespoon (15 ml) Dijon mustard
juice of ½ lime
1 bunch green asparagus
1 oz. (25 g) Parmesan shavings
salt and white pepper

Wash the radishes and slice them thinly.

In a skillet, lightly color the walnuts in the grapeseed oil. Set aside a few walnuts for garnish, and finely chop the others. In a small bowl, combine the chopped nuts, cream, mustard, and lime juice. Season with salt and pepper.

Peel the lower part of the asparagus stems. Cook them briefly in 3 pints (1 ½ liters) boiling salted water.

Arrange the asparagus on individual plates with 2 tablespoons (30 ml) rémoulade and a handful of radish slices. Sprinkle with the remaining walnuts and Parmesan shavings.

Éric Kayser's tip

This recipe is a refreshing side dish for tasty fish recipes, such as Buckwheat with Mackerel and Beets (see recipe p. 48).

CALF'S LIVER WITH SAUTÉED JERUSALEM ARTICHOKES AND WALNUTS

Serves 4
Preparation time: 20 minutes
Cooking time: 40 minutes

Ingredients

1 lb (450 g) calf's liver
¾ lb (350 g) Jerusalem artichokes
3 tablespoons (40 g) salted butter
1 tablespoon (15 ml) grapeseed oil
¼ cup (60 ml) balsamic vinegar
¾ cup (80 g) walnuts
pepper to taste

Ask your butcher to cut the calf's liver into slices just under 1 inch (2 cm) thick.

Wash the Jerusalem artichokes and cook them for 30 minutes in 5 pints (2 ½ liters) boiling salted water. They should be cooked through but retain their firmness. Drain, setting aside a scant ½ cup (100 ml) of the cooking liquid. Peel the Jerusalem artichokes and cut into slices ¼ inch (5 mm) thick.

In a large skillet, over high heat, melt 1 ½ tablespoons (20 g) butter with the grapeseed oil. Sear the calf's liver on both sides. Season with pepper and deglaze with the balsamic vinegar. Set aside, keeping warm.

Melt the rest of the butter in the same skillet with the scant ½ cup (100 ml) reserved cooking liquid. Bring to the boil and add the Jerusalem artichoke slices. Incorporate the walnuts. Reduce, stirring constantly, until only a few spoonfuls of sauce remain.

Cut the calf's liver into strips of about 1 ¼ inch (3 cm) and add them to the skillet.

Serve immediately with white rice.

Éric Kayser's tip
Substitute half the Jerusalem artichokes with turnips.

MELON, PECAN, AND RED ONION COCKTAIL

Serves 4
Preparation time: 15 minutes
Cooking time: 15 minutes

Ingredients

1 cantaloupe melon
2 red onions
3 tablespoons plus 1 teaspoon (50 ml) olive oil
⅓ cup (90 ml) balsamic vinegar
½ cup (65 g) pecans
½ bunch tarragon
fleur de sel
crushed pepper

Peel and seed the melon. Cut it into 16 slices lengthways and chill.

Preheat the oven to 425°F (210°C).

Peel the onions and cut them into quarters. Drizzle them with a little olive oil and 4 tablespoons balsamic vinegar and season with salt and pepper.
Broil in the oven for 10 minutes. Add the pecans and continue broiling for 5 minutes.

Wash and dry the tarragon leaves.

Divide the chilled melon, pecans, and hot onions into 4 bowls, and drizzle with the remaining vinegar. Garnish with the tarragon and serve immediately.

Éric Kayser's tip

Serve this hot and cold salad in Martini glasses, pouring 1 teaspoon (5 ml) Chartreuse liqueur into each glass.

SALTED ALMONDS
WITH KIWI

Serves 4
Preparation time: 10 minutes
Cooking time: 30 minutes

Ingredients
½ cup (100 g) salt
⅓ cup (50 g) almonds
6 kiwis
2 tablespoons (30 ml) lemon juice

Preheat the oven to 350°F (180°C).

In a small saucepan, bring 2 cups (500 ml) water to the boil. Add the salt. Stir through until the salt has dissolved. Dip the almonds into the liquid and then place them on a baking tray. Roast for 30 minutes. They should be crunchy and lightly coated in salt.

Peel the kiwis and dice them into 1 inch (2.5 cm) cubes. Pour over the lemon juice.

Mix the almonds and kiwis together at the last moment to retain the textures of the ingredients.

Éric Kayser's tip
Try this snack with cocktails. It's good with dry white wine like Sauvignon Blanc or dry Riesling.

RED MULLET
WITH ALMOND SCALES

Serves 4
Preparation time: 15 minutes
Cooking time: 20 minutes

Ingredients
8 x 4 oz. (120 g) mullet
⅓ cup (75 ml) olive oil
3 oz. (80 g) slivered almonds
2 tomatoes
salt and pepper
fleur de sel
white pepper

Ask your fishmonger to fillet the fish.

In a skillet, heat 2 tablespoons (30 ml) of the olive oil and lightly color
the slivered almonds.

Allow them to cool.
Plunge the tomatoes into boiling water. Peel them, remove the seeds,
and dice the flesh. Combine with the almonds and season with salt and pepper.
Heat the rest of the olive oil in a skillet and rapidly panfry the fish fillets on both sides.
Season with fleur de sel and white pepper.

At the last minute, arrange 4 mullet fillets on each plate with 2 tablespoons
of almond "scales."

Éric Kayser's tip
For a balanced meal, fill bowls with Pasta with Basil and Sun-Dried Tomatoes (see recipe
p. 124), using slivered almonds instead of pine nuts, and serve the fillets on top.

115

BRIOCHE
WITH PINK PRALINES

Yield: 6 brioches
Total preparation time: 25 minutes
Chilling time: overnight
Total resting time: 3 hours
Baking time: 15 minutes

Ingredients

2 ½ cups (250 g) flour
1 teaspoon (5 g) salt
¼ cup (45 g) granulated sugar
½ cake (12.5 g) compressed yeast
1 ½ oz. (40 g) starter (see recipe p. 94)
5 eggs
½ cup (125 g) butter
½ teaspoon (3 g) vanilla extract
2 ½ oz. (75 g) pink pralines
(from specialty stores)

Ensure that the ingredients are chilled so that the dough is not too warm after kneading is done.

A day ahead

Place the flour, salt, sugar, yeast, starter, and 4 of the eggs in the bowl of a food processor, avoiding direct contact of the salt and yeast. Process for 5 minutes. Knead for a further 6 minutes at higher speed. Gradually add the butter.

Set a few pralines aside for decoration. Switch back to lowest speed to finish kneading, adding the vanilla and pink pralines. Stop when the dough is completely homogenous.

Knead the dough into a ball and leave to rest for 40 minutes. Cover in plastic wrap and chill overnight.

To make the brioche

Remove the dough from the refrigerator 20 minutes ahead of time. Divide it into 6 equal portions (they should weigh about 2 oz. or 50 g each). Flatten them with the palm of your hand, without applying too much pressure, to make disks. Knead them into balls and allow to rest for 20 minutes.

Line a baking tray with parchment paper and place the brioches on this.
Cover with a damp dishcloth and allow to rise for 2 hours at room temperature.

Preheat the oven to 325°F (160°C).
Beat the remaining egg and brush the brioches with a pastry brush.
Place the reserved pieces of pink praline on top. Bake for 15 minutes.

Éric Kayser's tip

Pour 1 teaspoon (5 ml) almond liqueur over the warm brioches just before serving.

BITTER ALMOND BLANCMANGE
WITH STRAWBERRY COULIS

Serves 4
Preparation time: 10 minutes
Chilling time: 3 hours
Cooking time: 10 minutes

Ingredients

2 sheets (4 g) gelatin
⅔ cup (150 ml) whipping cream
⅔ cup (150 ml) orgeat (almond) syrup or almond milk
½ lb (250 g) strawberries
¼ cup (50 g) brown sugar

Soak the gelatin sheets in very cold water for a few minutes and drain well.

In a saucepan, bring the whipping cream and the orgeat syrup to the boil, and remove immediately from the heat. Incorporate the sheets of gelatin and pour the mixture into individual bowls.

Wash the strawberries and process them with the brown sugar to make a coulis. Chill for at least 3 hours.

Pour the strawberry coulis over the blancmanges and serve.

Éric Kayser's tip

When other berries—raspberries, wild strawberries, and redcurrants—are in season, add them to the coulis.

SPANISH-STYLE MUSSELS WITH MINT AND PINE NUTS

Serves 4
Preparation time: 15 minutes
Cooking time: 10 minutes

Ingredients

24 Spanish or other large mussels
½ cup or 2 ½ oz. (70 g) pine nuts
½ bunch mint
¼ cup (50 g) butter
salt and pepper

Preheat the oven to 350°F (180°C).

Using a knife, open the mussels (or ask your fishmonger). Remove one half of the shell, leaving the mussel attached to the other half.

Place the pine nuts in a baking tray and roast them lightly.

Wash and dry the mint leaves. Chop them finely and blend them with the butter. Incorporate the pine nuts. Season with salt and pepper. Generously stuff the mussels, and place them on the baking tray. Cook for 5 minutes in the preheated oven.

Serve hot.

Éric Kayser's tip
Give these mussels an even more pronounced Spanish taste by adding 1 oz. (25 g) diced spicy chorizo to the stuffing.

PASTA WITH BASIL
AND SUN-DRIED TOMATOES

Serves 4
Preparation time: 15 minutes
Cooking time: 10 minutes

Ingredients

1 tablespoon plus 1 teaspoon
(20 ml) olive oil
½ cup or 2 ½ oz. (70 g) pine nuts
4 oz. (120 g) sun-dried tomatoes in oil
⅓ cup (60 g) grated Parmesan
1 bunch basil
1 lb (500 g) penne pasta
salt and pepper

In a small skillet, heat the olive oil. Color the pine nuts slightly. Blend half the pine nuts with the dried tomatoes and their oil. Incorporate just over half the Parmesan cheese.

Wash and dry the basil leaves. Snip finely.

In a large pot, cook the penne, using 8 pints (4 liters) boiling salted water, following the instructions on the package.

Mix the penne with the purée of pine nuts and dried tomatoes.

Sprinkle the remaining pine nuts and Parmesan cheese, and the snipped basil, over the plates. Season with salt and pepper.

Éric Kayser's tip
Serve this dish in well-heated soup plates.

SALMON, TOMATO, AND FENNEL RAVIOLES

Serves 4
Preparation time: 20 minutes
Cooking time: 35 minutes

Ingredients
3 tomatoes
2 tablespoons (25 ml) olive oil
¼ cup (40 g) pine nuts
½ lb (250 g) fennel
½ lemon
8 thin slices smoked salmon
(¾ lb or 360 g)
fleur de sel
pepper

Preheat the oven to 425°F (210°C).

Wash the tomatoes and cut each one into 6 pieces. Drizzle with 1 tablespoon (15 ml) olive oil, and season with fleur de sel and pepper. Broil them on a baking tray for 15 minutes.

In a small skillet, heat the rest of the olive oil and lightly color the pine nuts.

Wash the fennel and cut it into small cubes. Place them, together with the half lemon, in a small saucepan. Cover with salted water. Cook for 15 minutes. The fennel should retain its firmness but be tender. Remove the half lemon and drain the fennel.

Chop the tomato slices and combine with the fennel and pine nuts. Season with pepper. Using a cookie cutter, cut out a 4 inch (10 cm) diameter disk from each slice of salmon.

Place a disk of salmon on each plate, add 1 tablespoon of the fennel preparation, and cover with another disk of salmon to make 8 ravioles.

Éric Kayser's tip
Enjoy this dish for special occasions with a glass of blanc de blanc champagne.

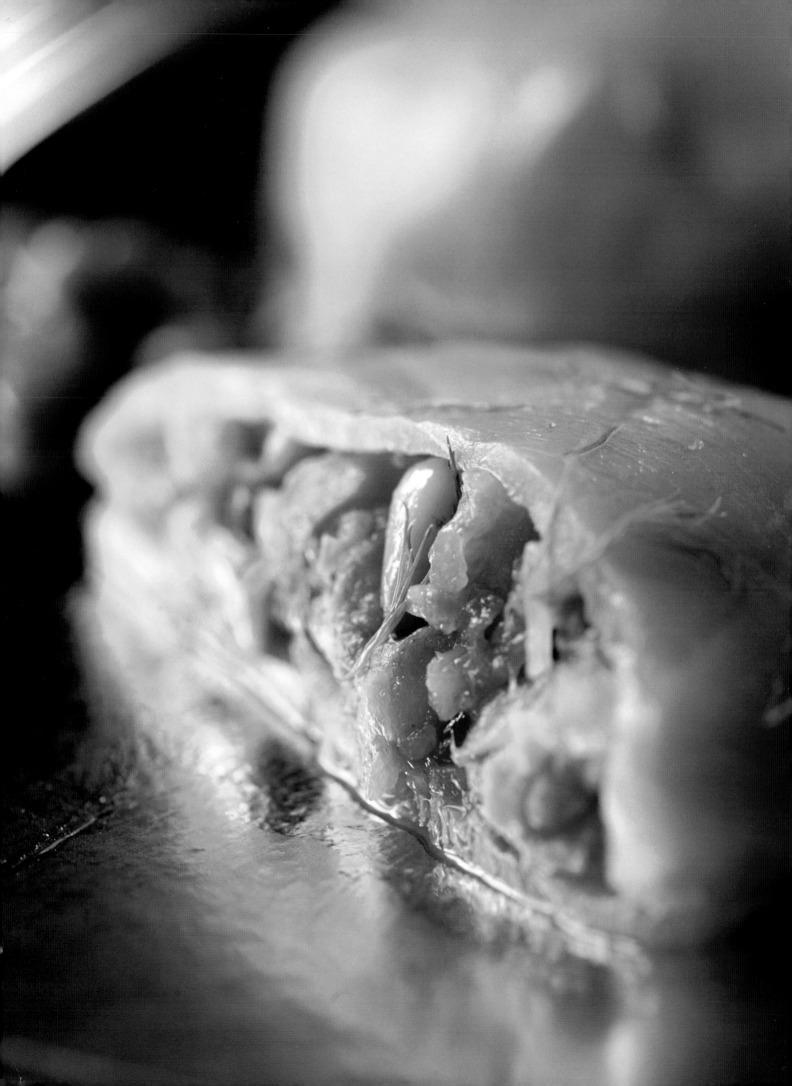

PINE NUT
AND PINE HONEY LOAF

Yields 2 loaves
Preparation time: 15 minutes
Baking time: 30 minutes

Ingredients

1 cup (250 g) butter, softened
⅔ cup (125 g) granulated sugar
½ cup (185 g) pine or other dark honey
2 ½ cups (250 g) all-purpose flour
1 ¼ teaspoons (5 g) baking powder
3 eggs
1 cup (150 g) pine nuts

Preheat the oven to 350°F (180°C).

Using an electric beater, beat the butter, sugar, and ⅓ cup (125 g) honey. Mix together the flour and baking powder in a separate bowl. Add the eggs one by one to the butter mixture, and then add the flour and baking powder. Delicately stir in the pine nuts using a spatula or wooden spoon.

Pour the batter into 2 loaf pans and bake for 30 minutes, until golden brown. The loaves are done when a cake tester comes out dry.

In a small saucepan, heat the remaining 2 ½ tablespoons (60 g) honey with 3 tablespoons (45 ml) water.

As soon as you remove the loaves from the oven, brush them with the honey icing using a pastry brush.

Éric Kayser's tip
These loaves keep very well. Cover them in plastic wrap as soon as they cool.

BAGUETTE TURNOVERS FILLED WITH GOAT CHEESE AND TOMATOES

Serves 4
Preparation time: 15 minutes
Cooking time: 15 minutes

Ingredients

2 tomatoes
4 x 2 oz. (60 g) bread rolls
4 teaspoons (20 ml) olive oil
5 oz. (150 g) fresh goat cheese
½ cup (125 g) plain yoghurt (without gelatin)
⅓ cup (50 g) sultanas
a few summer savory flowers
salt and white pepper

Preheat the oven to 325°F (160°C).

Wash the tomatoes and cut them into quarters. Peel them and remove the seeds.

Cut the tops off the bread rolls and set aside the lids. Hollow out a little of the soft part. Grease the inside of the rolls and the lids with oil. Place on a rack and toast in the oven for 5 minutes.

Remove the rolls and raise the oven temperature to 350°F (170°C).

Combine the goat cheese, yoghurt, and sultanas. Season with salt and pepper.
Fill the bread rolls with the mixture, adding the tomato slices. Bake for 10 minutes.

Replace the lids of the bread on the turnovers and decorate with summer savory flowers. Serve immediately.

Éric Kayser's tip
I like to serve these sweet-savory turnovers as a pre-dinner snack with celery and bell pepper sticks.

MILDLY SPICED CARROT
AND RAISIN CASSEROLE

Serves 4
Preparation time: 15 minutes
Cooking time: 25 minutes

Ingredients
10 oz. (300 g) carrots
1 stick cinnamon
1 star anise
black pepper
1 dried lemon (from specialty stores)
3 tablespoons (40 g) brown sugar
3 ½ tablespoons (50 ml) dry white wine
⅓ cup (60 g) raisins

Wash the carrots and peel them. Slice them thinly (less than ¼ inch or 0.5 cm).

In a small saucepan, heat the spices (cinnamon, star anise, and pepper), the dried lemon, and brown sugar for 5 minutes. Pour in the wine to make a syrup. Add the carrots and lower the heat. Put in the raisins and cover the saucepan. Simmer for 20 minutes.

Stir from time to time with a wooden spoon.

Remove the cinnamon and star anise before serving.

Éric Kayser's tip
Serve these sweet, mildly spiced vegetables as a side with a flavorsome meat dish like Calf's Liver with Sautéed Jerusalem Artichokes and Walnuts (see recipe p. 108).

COCONUT MILK RICE PUDDING WITH RAISINS

Serves 4
Preparation time: 15 minutes
Cooking time: 35 minutes

Ingredients

1 vanilla pod
½ lb (250 g) Arborio or other round rice
1 ⅔ cup (400 ml) coconut milk
1 scant cup (200 ml) whole milk
¾ cup (150 g) brown sugar
¾ cup or 3 oz. (100 g) raisins
zest and juice of ½ unsprayed or organic lime
1 egg yolk, beaten

Split the vanilla pod lengthways using the tip of a sharp knife.

Rapidly rinse the rice. In a saucepan, heat the coconut milk, whole milk, and brown sugar. Add the rice and the two vanilla pod halves. Simmer for 25 minutes, stirring frequently, until the mixture is creamy.

Add the raisins and the lime zest and juice. Incorporate the beaten egg yolk. Spoon into large bowls or tall glasses.

Éric Kayser's tip

If you're serving this dessert to adults, soak the raisins in a tablespoon (20 ml) of rum.

DRIED PLUM
AND LAMB TIDBITS

Serves 4
Preparation time: 15 minutes
Cooking time: 10 minutes

Ingredients
20 dried plums
1 bunch summer savory
7 oz. (200 g) ground meat,
preferably lamb
1 shallot, snipped
salt and pepper

Preheat the oven to 350°F (180°C).

Remove the pits from the dried plums, without cutting them right through, to form a tube shape.

Wash and dry the summer savory leaves. If there are any flowers, set them aside.

Mix the ground meat with the shallot and summer savory leaves. Season with salt and pepper. Fill the dried plums and pierce them with small wooden skewers.

Cover a baking tray with parchment paper. Place the skewers on this and cook for 10 minutes.

Éric Kayser's tip
Serve these tidbits with a bowl of plain yoghurt or buttermilk for dipping.

DRIED PLUM
AND ZUCCHINI SANDWICHES

Serves 4
Preparation time: 20 minutes
Cooking time: 15 minutes

Ingredients

generous ⅓ cup or 2 oz. (50 g)
pitted dried plums
⅓ cup or 2 ½ oz. (70 g) salted ricotta
4 small zucchini
1 tablespoon plus 1 teaspoon
(20 ml) olive oil
4 slices cured ham
salt and pepper

Preheat the oven to 350°F (180°C).

Chop the dried plums finely and combine with the ricotta.

Cut the zucchini in half lengthways. Drizzle with olive oil. Season with salt and pepper. Arrange them on a baking tray, cut side downward. Broil for 10 minutes. Leave the oven switched on.

Cut the slices of cured ham into 3 lengthways to make fine strips.

Spread the dried plum mixture on half a zucchini and cover with the other half. Roll three strips of ham around each zucchini sandwich. Heat the sandwiches in the oven for 5 minutes just before serving.

Éric Kayser's tip
Replace the zucchini with peeled, roasted bell peppers to make rolls instead of sandwiches.

DRIED PLUM CLAFOUTIS

Serves 4
Preparation time: 15 minutes
Baking time: 40 minutes

Ingredients

1 scant cup (200 ml) milk
2 egg yolks
1 oz. (30 g) vanilla flan mix (from
specialty stores)
⅓ cup or 1 oz. (30 g) ground almonds
2 whole eggs
1 cup (250 ml) heavy cream
or crème fraîche
2 tablespoons (30 ml) dried plum liqueur
⅔ cup or 4 oz. (120 g) granulated sugar
⅔ cup or 3 oz. (100 g)
pitted dried plums

Preheat the oven to 350°F (180°C).

Combine the milk and egg yolks.

Whisk together the flan mix and ground almonds. Stir these ingredients into the milk-yolk mixture, and add the 2 whole eggs.

Add the cream and liqueur. Mix delicately, adding the sugar.

Line a baking dish with parchment paper and arrange the dried plums on it. Carefully pour the batter over the dried plums and bake for about 40 minutes, until the clafoutis is firm.

Éric Kayser's tip

I love the smells, so reminiscent of old-fashioned baking, that spread through the house while this cake bakes.

OREGANO-FLAVORED FIG
AND CHERRY TOMATO SALAD

Serves 4
Preparation time: 15 minutes

Ingredients
½ lb (200 g) dried figs
1 lb (400 g) cherry tomatoes
2 tablespoons plus 1 teaspoon
(35 ml) olive oil
juice of 1 tangerine
3 tablespoons (45 ml) lemon juice
1 bunch oregano
fleur de sel and crushed long pepper

Finely slice the dried figs.

Wash the cherry tomatoes. Take 10 oz. (300 g) tomatoes and cut them in half.
In a food processor, blend the remaining tomatoes with the olive oil, tangerine juice, and lemon juice.

Wash and dry the oregano leaves.

In a large salad bowl, combine the figs and tomato halves with the citrus vinaigrette.

Garnish with the oregano leaves. Season with salt and pepper.

Éric Kayser's tip
Try to find Turkish dried figs for this recipe—they are particularly tasty.

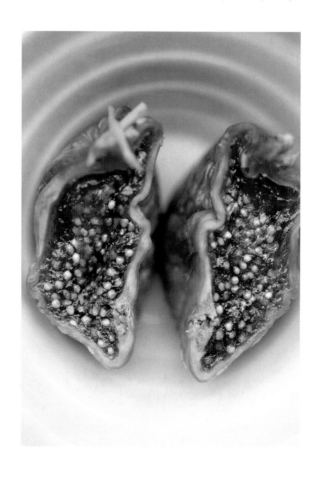

FIG BREAD, APPLES,
AND DUCK BREAST TAPAS

Serves 4
Preparation time: 20 minutes
Cooking time: 10 minutes

Ingredients

2 Royal Gala apples
juice and zest of ½ organic lemon
1 x ½ lb (230 g) fig bread, sliced
7 oz. (200 g) smoked duck breast, sliced
fleur de sel
crushed pepper

Wash the apples. Quarter them and remove the pips.

Cut each quarter into thin slices ¼ inch thick (0.5 cm). Pour over the lemon juice and zest. Toast the fig bread slices, and cut each slice into 3.

Fry the duck breast slices in a skillet without adding any fat (the fat that exudes will be enough). Allow them to cool for a few minutes, then combine them with the apple slices and pieces of toast. Season with salt and pepper.

Éric Kayser's tip

If you can't find fig bread, use country bread and sauté 1 ½ oz. (45 g) snipped dried figs with the duck breast.

CHICKEN LIVERS AND FRENCH BEANS WITH CREAMED FIG SAUCE

Serves 4
Preparation time: 20 minutes
Cooking time: 25 minutes

Ingredients

1 lb (500 g) chicken livers
2 oz. (60 g) dried figs
⅔ cup (150 ml) dry white wine,
preferably a Riesling
1 ½ tablespoons (20 g) butter
5 g barberries or pink peppercorns
½ lb (250 g) thin French beans
1 tablespoon (15 ml) olive oil
fleur de sel
pepper

Clean the chicken livers and separate the two lobes (or ask your butcher).

Finely dice the figs. In a saucepan, bring a scant ½ cup (100 ml) of the wine and the same quantity of water to the boil. Put the chopped figs into the liquid and lower the heat. When the figs have completely disintegrated and the mixture has a creamy consistency, remove from the heat and add 1 teaspoon (5 g) butter and the barberries. Season with salt.

In a large pot, blanch the beans in boiling water.

In a large skillet, heat the oil and the rest of the butter and panfry the chicken livers. Deglaze with the remaining white wine. Season with salt and pepper.

Divide the French beans between 4 plates and place the chicken livers on top. Spoon over the creamed fig sauce.

Éric Kayser's tip
Heighten the flavor of the sauce by using a scant ½ cup (100 ml) chicken broth instead of water.

WHITING COATED IN CHESTNUT FLOUR
WITH PURPLE POTATOES

Serves 4
Preparation time: 20 minutes
Total cooking time: 35 minutes

Ingredients
4 x ½ lb (250 g) whiting
10 oz. (300 g) small purple
vitelotte potatoes
1 tablespoon (15 ml) olive oil
4 eggs, separated
4 oz. (120 g) chestnut flour
2 ½ tablespoons (40 ml) grapeseed oil
4 tablespoons (60 ml) lemon juice
fleur de sel
salt and pepper

Ask your fishseller to fillet the whiting.

Preheat the oven to 400°F (200°C).

Wash the potatoes and drizzle them with the olive oil. Sprinkle with fleur de sel and pepper. Cook them on a baking tray for 25 minutes.

Add a pinch of salt and a little pepper to the egg whites and beat them stiffly.

Beat the yolks with 1 ½ oz. (50 g) chestnut flour and incorporate the beaten egg whites. Coat the whiting fillets with the remaining chestnut flour and shake off any excess. Dip them in the egg mixture.

Heat the grapeseed oil in a skillet and fry the fillets on both sides.

Spoon lemon juice over the fish before serving, and accompany with the potatoes as a side dish.

Éric Kayser's tip
For a more pronounced "fish and chips" taste, use vinegar instead of lemon juice.

SWEET-AND-SOUR SALMON AND CHESTNUT KEBABS

Serves 4
Preparation time: 20 minutes
Chilling time: overnight
Cooking time: 8 minutes

Ingredients

½ **bunch baby onions**
1 lb (480 g) **salmon fillets**
4 oz. (120 g) **whole canned**
chestnuts in brine
4 tablespoons (60 ml) **rice vinegar**
2 tablespoons (30 ml) **soy sauce**
1 teaspoon **grated fresh ginger**

Wash the onions and slice them finely.

Cut the salmon into 1 inch (2.5 cm) cubes.

Drain the chestnuts and reserve the brine. Combine the brine with the rice vinegar, soy sauce, and grated ginger.

Thread the salmon cubes alternated with the chestnuts onto 8 wooden skewers. Pour over half the chestnut vinegar, and marinate for 1 hour in the refrigerator.

Preheat the oven to 425°F (210°C) in "broil" position.

Mix the sliced onions with the other half of the chestnut vinaigrette.

Line a baking tray with parchment paper and place the kebabs on the tray. Cook for 5 to 8 minutes, depending on how well done you like your salmon. Spoon over the vinaigrette.

Éric Kayser's tip

For multicolored kebabs, alternate the salmon cubes with cubes of tuna and cod.
In this case, allow 5–6 oz. (160 g) of each type of fish.

CHESTNUT BREAD
WITH APRICOTS AND PISTACHIOS

Serves 4
Preparation time: 15 minutes
Marinating time: 3 hours
Total cooking time: 10 minutes

Ingredients

12 fresh apricots
3 ½ tablespoons (45 g) brown sugar
1 tablespoon (15 ml) Armagnac
3 tablespoons (45 ml) heavy cream
or crème fraîche
3 oz. (80 g) crème de marrons—chestnut
cream (from specialty stores)
1 x ½ lb (230 g) chestnut loaf, sliced
1 oz. (25 g) chopped pistachios

Cut the apricots in half and remove the pits. Combine the halves with the sugar and Armagnac. Leave to marinate at room temperature for 3 hours.

Preheat the oven to 325°F (160°C).

Whisk the heavy cream with the chestnut cream.

Toast the bread and spread with the cream. Top with the marinated apricots and sprinkle with chopped pistachios. Grill in the oven for 5 minutes.

Serve with a scoop of pistachio ice cream.

Éric Kayser's tip

When apricots aren't in season, I use pink grapefruit segments.

RECIPE INDEX

Side Dishes

Desserts

Acknowledgments

My warm thanks go to all the members
of the team who helped me create this book:
Yaïr Yosefi, Clay McLachlan, and Julien Desrée
as well as to all our suppliers
Hugo Desnoyer
Joël Thiébault
Pasta Line
Dominique Maury Fishmongers
Déroche Company
Mr. Khaled
Sens Gourmet
Ercuis & Raynaud